THE

Series MGA 1600
DRIVER'S HANDBOOK

A copy of this Driver's Handbook is sent out with every M.G. (Series MGA 1600) car. Additional copies are obtainable only from your M.G. Distributor and Part No. AKD 1172 C should be quoted when ordering.

Published by
THE M.G. CAR COMPANY LIMITED
Proprietors: Morris Motors Limited
ABINGDON-ON-THAMES
Telephone: Abingdon 251-2-3-4   *Telegrams:* Emgee, Abingdon

Sole Exporters
NUFFIELD EXPORTS LIMITED
Proprietors: Morris Motors Limited
COWLEY - OXFORD - ENGLAND
Phone: Oxford, England, 77733   *Telex:* 83133 Morex, Oxford, England
Cables: Morex, Oxford, England

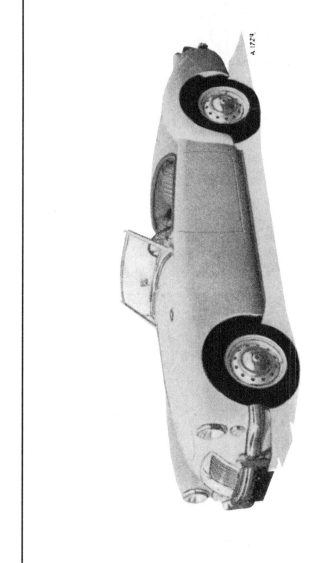

THE M.G. (SERIES MGA 1600) TWO-SEATER (L.H.D. MODEL)

FOREWORD

THE information contained in this Driver's Handbook has been confined to the essentials necessary for the proper running and driving of the car. Nevertheless, the owner will find all the information required to maintain the car in first-class condition and to enable him to give it those all-important items of attention which go so far to ensure trouble-free and satisfactory service.

Every M.G. car leaving the Works is capable of giving absolute satisfaction if attention is given to the essential maintenance operations detailed in this book. Remember that M.G. Distributors/Dealers are better equipped to provide routine and repair service than the owner-driver; therefore, if you encounter trouble consult the Distributor or Dealer—they are at your service.

For those requiring information of a more detailed and technical nature than is contained in the Driver's Handbook a Workshop Manual is available at a reasonable price from your Distributor or Dealer.

IDENTIFICATION

When communicating with the Company or your Distributor/Dealer always quote the car and engine numbers; the registration number is of no use and is not required.

Note that all correspondence concerning exported cars must be addressed to Nuffield Exports Limited.

Car number. Stamped on a plate mounted on the engine bulkhead shelf.

Engine number. On a metal plate fixed to the right-hand side of the cylinder block.

The engine number comprises a series of letters and numbers, presenting, in code, the capacity, make, and type of unit, ancillaries fitted, and the type of compression, together with the serial number of the unit.

The major components of this vehicle also have serial numbers, and should it be necessary to quote them at any time, they will be found in the following locations:

Gearbox. Stamped on the top of the gearbox to the left of the dipstick and filler plug.

Rear axle. Stamped on the front of the axle tube on the left-hand side adjacent to the spring seat.

Body. Stamped on a metal plate fixed to the bulkhead and situated between the right-hand bonnet hinge and the fuse unit.

GENERAL DATA

Engine	4-cylinder overhead-valve
Bore	2·968 in. (75·39 mm.)
Stroke	3·5 in. (88·9 mm.)
Capacity	1588 c.c. (96·9 cu. in.)
Compression ratio	8·3 : 1
Firing order	1, 3, 4, 2
Valve clearance .. .. ,. ..	·015 in. (·38 mm.) (hot)
Sparking plugs	Champion N5 (formerly NA8), 14 mm., ¾ in. reach
Sparking plug gap	·025 in. (·64 mm.)
Ignition timing	7° B.T.D.C.
Contact breaker gap	·014 to ·016 in. (·36 to ·41 mm.)
Rear axle ratio	4·3 : 1
Overall gear ratios: First	15·652 : 1
Second	9·520 : 1
Third	5·908 : 1
Fourth	4·3 : 1
Reverse	20·468 : 1
Tyre size	5·60—15

Tyre pressures:

Normal	Front: 17 lb./sq. in. (1·2 kg./cm.²) Rear: 20 lb./sq. in. (1·4 kg./cm.²)
Full load or fast driving	Front: 21 lb./sq. in. (1·48 kg./cm.²) Rear: 24 lb./sq. in. (1·69 kg./cm.²)
Competition work, sustained high- speed driving	Front: 23 lb./sq. in. (1·62 kg./cm.²) Rear: 26 lb./sq. in. (1·83 kg./cm.²)

Dimensions:

	Disc wheels	Wire wheels
Track—front	3 ft. 11½ in. (1·206 m.)	3 ft. 11⅞ in. (1·216 m.)
Track—rear	4 ft. 0¾ in. (1·238 m.)	4 ft. 0¾ in. (1·238 m.)
Turning circle	30 ft. 6 in. (9·3 m.)	
Toe-in	Nil	
Wheelbase	7 ft. 10 in. (2·388 m.)	
Length (overall)	13 ft. 0 in. (3·96 m.)	
Width (overall)	4 ft. 10 in. (1·45 m.)	
Height (overall)	4 ft. 2 in. (1·27 m.)	
Ground clearance	6 in. (15·24 cm.)	
Unladen weight (ready for road) ..	18 cwt. (914 kg.)	

Capacities:

Fuel tank	10 gal. (45·4 litres, 12 U.S. gal.)
Cooling system	10 pints (5·67 litres, 12 U.S. pints)
Engine sump (including filter) ..	8 pints (4·54 litres, 9½ U.S. pints)
Gearbox	4 pints (2·27 litres, 4¾ U.S. pints)
Rear axle	2 pints (1·14 litres, 2·4 U.S. pints)

Lamp bulbs—see page 30

NOTE.—References to right or left hand in this Handbook are made when viewing the car from the rear.

CONTROLS

Gear lever

The four forward gears and the reverse gear are engaged by moving the lever to the positions indicated in the illustration inset below.

To engage the reverse gear move the lever to the left of the neutral position until resistance is felt, apply side pressure to the lever to overcome the resistance, and then pull it backwards to engage the gear.

Synchromesh engagement is provided on second, third, and fourth gears.

Ensure that the gear lever is in the neutral position before attempting to start the engine.

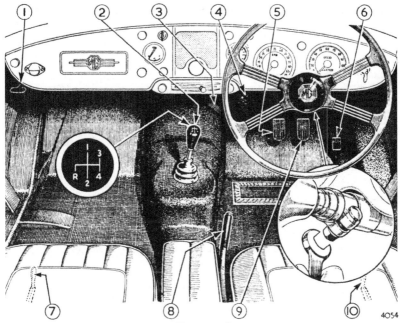

The controls

1. Bonnet release.
2. Gear lever.
3. Gearbox oil filler plug.
4. Headlamp dip switch.
5. Clutch pedal.
6. Accelerator.
7. Seat lock.
8. Hand brake lever.
9. Foot brake.
10. Seat lock.

Brake pedal

The centre pedal operates the hydraulic brakes on all four wheels and will also operate the twin stop warning lamps when the ignition is switched on.

Clutch pedal

The left-hand pedal operates the hydraulic clutch release. Do not allow the foot to rest on the clutch pedal while driving as this will cause excessive wear of the operating mechanism.

CONTROLS

Hand brake

The hand brake lever is located alongside the gearbox cover and operates the rear wheel brakes only.

To operate, pull up the lever and press the knob in the end with the thumb to lock the lever in position. To release the brakes, pull upwards on the lever to release the lock automatically and then push downwards.

Always apply the hand brake when parking.

Steering-column adjustment (optional extra)

The steering-column is adjustable for length. This enables the steering-wheel to be placed in the most comfortable driving position after slackening a clamp bolt below the wheel hub.

Always retighten the nut securely after adjustment. See the inset in the illustration on page 5.

Choke or mixture control

To enrich the mixture and assist starting when the engine is cold pull out the knob marked 'C' and lock it in position by turning it anti-clockwise.

Turn the knob clockwise and push it inwards to the normal running position as soon as the engine is warm enough to run without the rich mixture.

Never allow the engine to run for any length of time with the knob pulled out.

Bonnet lock release

The bonnet is hinged at the rear and the lock is released by pulling on the ring below the instrument panel on the extreme left-hand side of the car.

The bonnet is still held by the safety catch, which must be released before the bonnet can be raised (see page 14).

To relock the bonnet in the fully closed position after opening, press downwards on the front of the bonnet until the lock is heard to engage.

Seat adjustment

A lever is provided at the front of each seat and this must be pressed outwards to release the catches and allow the seat to slide.

The seat will lock in the desired position as the lever is released.

Door locks (Coupé only)

The door on the driver's side of both the left- and right-hand-drive two-seater coupé is locked from the outside of the car, using the ignition key. The passenger door is locked by lifting the interior door handle to its uppermost position. Push the handle downwards to unlock the door.

Ignition switch

Turn the ignition switch key clockwise to switch on the ignition. Do not leave it switched on when the engine is not running, except for very short periods.

The fuel pump and gauge are brought into action by this switch, which is also the master switch for the windshield wipers and direction indicators.

Without the removable key the engine cannot be started.

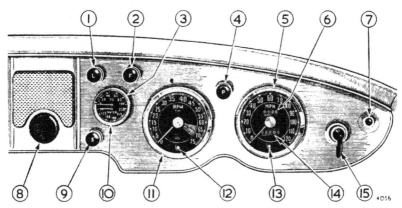

The instruments and switches

1. Headlamp and sidelamp switch.
2. Fog lamp switch.
3. Oil gauge.
4. Panel lamp switch.
5. Speedometer.
6. Trip mileage.
7. Flasher warning light.
8. Horn button.
9. Starter switch.
10. Water temperature gauge.
11. Revolution indicator.
12. Ignition warning light.
13. Headlamp beam warning light.
14. Total mileage.
15. Direction indicator switch.

Starter switch

Pull out the knob marked 'S' to operate the starter motor. The switch must be pulled out smartly and pushed in immediately the engine starts.

If the engine does not start at once, allow it to come to rest before using the switch again.

Lamp switch

To switch on the sidelamps, tail lamps, and number-plate illumination lamp pull out the knob marked 'L'.

Turn the knob clockwise and pull out again to switch on the headlamps.

See 'Headlamp beam dip switch' on page 8.

Fog lamp switch

A fog lamp is not fitted as standard equipment, but the switch marked 'F' on the instrument panel is connected to the battery and is ready for use when a fog lamp is connected to it.

Pull out the knob to switch on the fog lamp.

Horn button

This is the black button below the grille in the centre of the panel.

SWITCHES

Panel lamp switch

To illuminate the instruments turn the control knob 'P' clockwise. The first movement of the knob will switch on the lamps, and further turning to the right will dim the lamps.

The panel lamps will operate only when the sidelamps are also switched on.

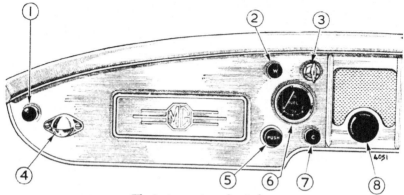

The instruments and switches

1. Map-reading lamp switch.
2. Windshield wiper switch.
3. Ignition switch.
4. Map-reading lamp.

5. Windshield washer control.
6. Fuel gauge.
7. Choke control.
8. Horn button.

Direction indicator switch

The lever-type switch on the outer edge of the panel controls the flashing indicator unit. The unit will operate only while the ignition is switched on and flashes the sidelamp and tail lamp on the side of the car to which the switch lever is moved until it is automatically switched off.

While the flashing unit is switched on the warning light next to the switch will show green.

Windshield wiper switch

Pull out the control 'W' to set the wiper blades in motion. Push in the knob to switch off the motor and park the blades.

The windshield wipers are self-parking and operate only when the ignition is switched on.

Headlamp beam dip switch

This is situated to the left of the clutch pedal and is foot-operated. The switch will dip the headlamp beams on one depression and raise them on the next.

To give the driver clear indication when the headlamp beams may dazzle approaching drivers a warning light in the speedometer dial glows when the headlamp beams are in the raised position.

Map-reading lamp switch

The map-reading lamp is controlled by the adjacent knob, which must be pulled out to switch on the light. The lamp will only operate while the sidelamps are switched on.

Speedometer

In addition to indicating the speed of the car, the speedometer records the trip and total distances. The trip recorder enables the distance of a particular journey to be recorded and is reset to zero by pushing upwards the knob below the instrument and turning it anti-clockwise until the figures read zero.

Main beam warning light

The warning light at the bottom of the speedometer dial glows red when the headlamp main beams are in use as a reminder to dip the beams when approaching other traffic.

Engine revolution indicator

The speed of the engine is indicated by this dial, which is calibrated in hundreds of revolutions per minute. Normal use of the engine will not require speeds over 5,000 r.p.m. and great care must be taken if the needle does approach the amber sector of the dial, which commences at 5,500 r.p.m. Under favourable conditions the needle may be allowed to enter the amber sector, but **under no circumstances must it enter the red sector.**

Ignition warning light

The warning light at the bottom of the revolution indicator dial glows red when the ignition is switched on and will go out again when the engine is started and its speed is increased sufficiently for the dynamo to charge the battery. Should the light glow at all engine speeds, the dynamo is not charging the battery and the wiring circuit and dynamo drive belt should be examined immediately.

Do not leave the ignition switched on for more than a few moments while the engine is stationary.

Oil pressure gauge

The pressure of the oil in the engine lubricating system as shown on the gauge should be between 30 and 80 lb./sq. in. (2·1 and 5·6 kg./cm.²) under normal running conditions. Approximately 10 lb./sq. in. (·7 kg./cm.²) should be shown when the engine is idling.

Water temperature gauge

The temperature of the cooling water leaving the cylinder head is indicated by this gauge and should be approximately 160 to 190° F. (71 to 88° C.) when the engine is running normally. If the normal running temperature is greatly exceeded the cause must be traced and rectified immediately.

Fuel gauge

This operates only when the ignition is switched on and indicates the quantity of fuel in the tank.

OPTIONAL EQUIPMENT

Heating and ventilating

When the 2·75-kw. heating and demising unit is fitted fresh air is ducted from the radiator grille to the heating element and blower motor mounted below the bonnet. Water from the engine cooling system is used to heat the element.

Warmed air issues from the toeboard or the windshield demisting vents according to the position of the controls mounted below the instrument panel. In warm weather the controls may be set to provide unheated fresh air for ventilation.

1. Air control.   2. Blower switch and temperature control.   3. Demist control.

Air

The left-hand knob controls the air supply. When the knob is pushed in the air duct is open and air at atmospheric temperature will enter the car when it is in motion and will issue from the toeboard or demisting vents.

Air blower

Pull out knob marked 'B' on the temperature control lever to switch on the blower motor, if the ignition is switched on also, and this will increase the flow of air into the car and may be used to give a supply of air when the car is stationary or travelling at low speed. If the blower motor is switched off and the air control knob pulled outwards to close the air duct fresh air cannot enter the car from the toeboard or windshield vents.

Demist

The right-hand knob on the heater unit control panel operates a shutter in the panel above the gearbox cover. When the control is pushed into the normal position the shutter is open and most of the air from the unit will enter the car at the toeboard, while some will issue from the vents below the windshield. As the knob is pulled out the shutter closes and more air is delivered to the demisting vents, giving the maximum supply of air to the windshield. This is the demist position of the control and also the windshield defrost position when the heater is operating and the blower is switched on.

Temperature

The temperature lever operates the water valve on the engine. When the lever is in the left-hand position the hot water supply is cut off and air entering the car through the unit will not be heated. As the lever is moved to the right the water supply is increased until the maximum temperature is obtained.

As a general guide, here are some of the more frequently required positions.

(1) *No additional ventilation or heating.* Pull out the air control, push the temperature control to the left.

(2) *Hot weather.* Push in the air and demist controls. Move the temperature control to the left. To increase the supply of air switch on the blower motor.

(3) *Warm weather.* Set the controls as for hot weather. To increase the supply of air switch on the blower motor. To prevent mist forming on the windshield pull out the demist control partially.

(4) *Cold weather.* Place the air control in its normal position. Place the temperature lever according to the degree of heating required. Switch on the blower to increase the air supply (if demisting is required pull out the demist control).

(5) *Severe cold.* Move the temperature control to the right for maximum heating and pull out the demist control fully to give a maximum supply of hot air to the windshield. Switch on the blower motor to increase air flow.

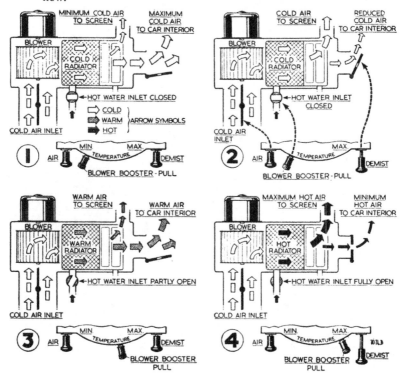

OPTIONAL EQUIPMENT

Windshield washer

The washing equipment supplied as an optional fitting is operated by pumping the knob on the instrument panel. As the knob moves towards the panel a jet of cleaning fluid is ejected onto the windshield from nozzles on the scuttle.

Set the windshield wipers in motion before operating the cleaning jets.

Pump the knob on the instrument panel to eject cleaning fluid onto the windshield

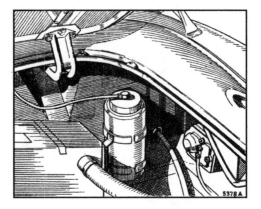

The unbreakable bottle in which the windshield washer fluid is stored

Windshield washer fluid

Fluid for the windshield is stored in an unbreakable bottle clipped to the engine bulkhead on the opposite side to the brake and clutch master cylinders. When refilling with fluid unscrew the cap from the bottle and lift the bottle from its clip.

Fitting the hard-top

The hard-top can be fitted either with or without the hood removed from the vehicle. If the hood is to be kept in the car, then it should be stowed away neatly prior to fitting the hard-top. The plated retaining brackets at the rear edge of the hard-top canopy should first be engaged with the anchor brackets (1) on the tonneau panel above the boot lid. Next, the hook-type side clips should be fitted over the hood frame pivot pins (2) and the knurled knobs screwed up lightly. Attach the front of the canopy by the method used to secure

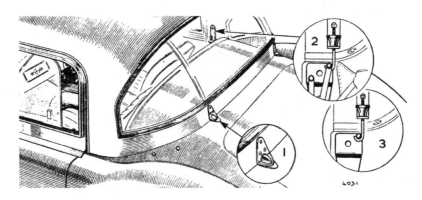

the folding hood, and after tightening the winged bolts the knurled knob on each side clip should also be fully tightened.

If the hood is not required it can be removed completely and special attachment brackets (available from an M.G. Distributor or Dealer) fitted in place of the hood frame pivot plates (3).

The following items of equipment are available as optional fittings:

Wire wheels.
White-walled tyres.
5·90—15 speed tyres.
Alternative axle ratio (4·55 : 1).
Adjustable steering-column (see page 6).
Tonneau cover.
Radiator blind (see page 18).
Heating and demisting equipment
  (see pages 10 and 11).
Twin horns.
Fog lamp (see page 7).
Cigar-lighter.

H.M.V. car radio (provision has
  been made for easy installation).
Windshield washer.
Detachable hard-top.
Competition windshield assembly.
Luggage carrier.
Wing driving mirror.
Cold air ventilation kit.
Ashtray.
Badge bar.
De-luxe sidescreens.

BODY DETAILS

Bonnet safety catch

After releasing the bonnet lock from inside the car (page 6) push back the safety catch and raise the bonnet.

Release the prop from the under side of the lid and place its end in the hole provided in the deflector above the fan blades.

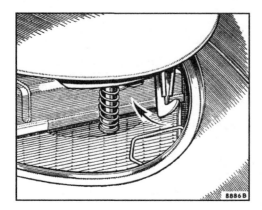

Release the bonnet lock from inside the car and push back the safety catch at the front of the bonnet

Pull the ring in the left-hand corner of the hood stowage compartment to release the boot lid

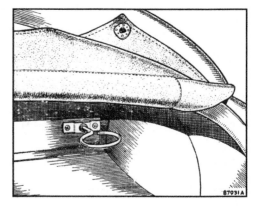

Opening the luggage boot

Tip forward the left-hand seat and pull the ring at the rear of the hood stowage compartment on the left-hand side.

Raise the boot lid and support it with the prop clipped to the under side.

To close the lid stow the prop and press down until the lock is heard to engage.

Filling the fuel tank

The quantity of fuel in the tank is indicated on the instrument panel and the filler cap is at the rear of the car on the right-hand side.

Lift the small lever on the cap to release and raise the cap. Press the cap downwards to close it.

Considerable loss of fuel can occur as a result of filling the fuel tank until the fuel is visible in the filler tube. If this is done and the vehicle is left in the sun, expansion due to heat will cause leakage with consequent loss of and danger from exposed fuel.

When filling up, therefore:

(1) Avoid filling the tank until the fuel is visible in the filler tube.

(2) If the tank is inadvertently overfilled, take care to park the vehicle in the shade and with the filler as high as possible.

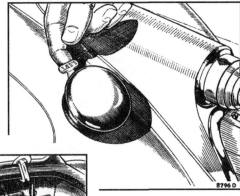

Lift the lever on the fuel tank filler to release the cap

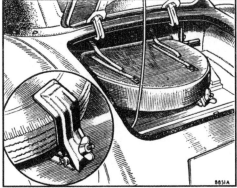

Unscrew the winged nut on the spare wheel clamp to release the wheel. Maintain the correct air pressure in the tyre

Spare wheel, starting handle, and tool kit

The spare wheel is housed in the luggage compartment and is clamped in position beneath the cover. Remember that the spare wheel tyre should be maintained at the normal running pressure of the rear tyres.

For tyre pressures see page 4.

The starting handle is located in spring clips above the spare wheel, with the tool roll strapped below it.

HIGH-SPEED TYRE PRESSURE CONDITIONS

The new British motorways and current facilities for Continental touring give the motorist many opportunities for driving at high and sustained high speeds. In such conditions, and in competition work, the tyres are subjected to greater stresses than those produced by ordinary driving.

Many factors, some probably as important as the physical characteristics of the tyre itself, affect the speed at which it should be driven: road surface, air temperature, and in particular the duration of high-speed driving. However, a normal tyre in good condition and at the correct pressure can be relied upon to perform satisfactorily at speeds up to 80 m.p.h. (128 km./hr.) and intermittently in excess of this by 10 m.p.h. (16 km./hr.). If the car is to be driven consistently at speeds near the maximum of which it is capable, special tyres should be fitted on the advice of the tyre manufacturers. The following tyre pressures should be adhered to:

	Front		Rear	
	lb./sq. in.	kg./cm.^{2}	lb./sq. in.	kg./cm.^{2}
Normal motoring	17	1·2	20	1·4
Fast motoring	21	1·48	24	1·69
Sustained high speeds and competition	23	1·62	26	1·83

These remarks do not apply to remoulded tyres since it is even more difficult to state with certainty what their maximum speed should be. Therefore, when it is intended to indulge in high speeds we advise the use of first-tread tyres.

RUNNING INSTRUCTIONS

Running-in speeds

The treatment given to a new car will have an important bearing on its subsequent life, and engine speeds during this early period must be limited.

The following instructions should be strictly adhered to:

During the first 500 miles (800 km.)

DO NOT exceed 45 m.p.h. (72 km.p.h.).

DO NOT operate at full throttle in any gear.

DO NOT allow the engine to labour in any gear.

Starting up

Before starting up the engine make sure that the gear lever is in the neutral position. When starting from cold pull out the choke or mixture control (marked 'C'). Switch on the ignition and operate the starter. The engine will be set in motion and after a second or two should start up, when the control must immediately be released. It is bad practice to keep the starter operating if the engine refuses to start as the starter takes a very heavy current from the batteries and may discharge them.

After the engine has run for a few minutes, or almost immediately in warm weather, the choke control should be pushed fully in. On no account must the engine be run for any length of time with this control pulled out or neat fuel will be drawn into the cylinders and considerable damage may be caused. The control should be returned to its normal position as soon as the engine is warm enough to run evenly without its use. It is not necessary, and in fact it is detrimental, to use the mixture or choke control when starting a warm engine.

Warming up

Research has proved that the practice of warming up an engine by allowing it to idle slowly is definitely harmful. The correct procedure is to let the engine run fairly fast, at approximately 1,000 r.p.m., so that it attains its correct working temperature **as quickly as possible.** Allowing the engine to work slowly in a cold state leads to excessive cylinder wear, and far less damage is done by driving the car straight on the road from cold than by letting the engine idle slowly in the garage.

COOLING SYSTEM

A pressurized cooling system is used on this vehicle and the pressure must be released gradually when removing the radiator filler cap when the system is hot. It is advisable to protect the hands against escaping steam and then turn the cap slowly anti-clockwise until the resistance of the safety stop is felt. Leave the cap in this position until all pressure is released. Press the cap downwards against the spring to clear the safety stops and continue turning until it can be lifted off.

Important

Never use a muff on the radiator grille to protect the cooling system in cold weather as this would seal the carburetter and heater unit air supply. The radiator must be protected by a blind such as the type available as an optional extra fitting.

Frost precautions

Water, when it freezes, expands, and if precautions are not taken there is considerable risk of bursting the radiator, cylinder block, or heater (where fitted). Such damage may be avoided by draining the cooling system when the vehicle is left for any length of time in frosty weather, or by adding anti-freeze to the water. When a heater is fitted anti-freeze **must** be used as no provision is made for draining the unit.

Before adding anti-freeze mixture the cooling system must be drained and flushed through by inserting a hose in the filling orifice and allowing water to flow through until clean. The taps should be closed after allowing all the water to drain away and the anti-freeze should be poured in first, followed by the water.

To avoid wastage by overflow add just sufficient water to cover the bottom of the header tank. Then run the engine until it is hot and add sufficient water to bring the surface to the correct working level, i.e. with about 1 in. (2·5 cm.) of water visible in the filler neck.

The cooling system is of the sealed type and relatively high temperatures are developed in the radiator header tank. For this reason anti-freeze solutions having an alcohol base are unsuitable owing to their high evaporation rate producing a rapid loss of coolant and a consequent interruption of circulation.

Only anti-freeze of the ethylene glycol type incorporating the correct type of corrosion inhibitor is suitable and owners are recommended to use Bluecol, Shell Snowflake, or Esso Anti-freeze. The use of any other anti-freeze that conforms to Specification B.S.3151 or B.S.3152 is also approved.

Do not use radiator anti-freeze solution in the windshield-washing equipment.

18

Filling the radiator

The radiator should be filled until approximately 1 in. (25 mm.) of water is visible in the filler neck.

Unscrew the filler cap slowly if it is being removed while the engine is hot.

The filler cap is retained by a bayonet catch with a graduated cam which permits release of internal pressure prior to removal. A lobe on the end of the cam guards against accidental release of the cap before the internal pressure is relieved. **Protect your hand against escaping steam.**

The radiator filler cap. Unscrew the cap slowly if it is being removed while the engine is hot

The radiator drain tap is located on the left-hand side of the radiator bottom tank. Access is gained from beneath the car

Radiator drain tap

This tap is located on the front of the radiator bottom tank on the left-hand side and is accessible from below the front bumper between the number-plate and the over-rider. Release the radiator filler cap carefully (see above) when draining the radiator. To drain the cooling system completely the engine drain tap must also be opened.

COOLING SYSTEM

Engine drain tap

To drain the water from the engine carefully release the radiator filler cap (see page 19) and open the tap on the rear right-hand side of the cylinder block.

To drain the cooling system completely the radiator drain tap also must be opened.

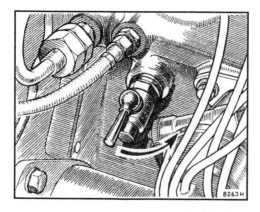

The cylinder block drain tap is located on the right-hand side of the engine at the rear

Anti-freeze mixture must be used when a heater is fitted as the cooling system cannot be completely drained

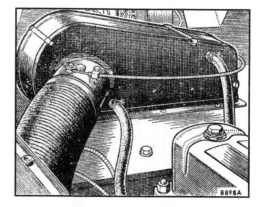

Heater unit

When a heater unit is fitted the water cannot be drained from it completely by opening the engine and radiator drain taps, and it is essential that an anti-freeze mixture is used in the cooling system to prevent damage by freezing.

To assist draining the system when a heater unit is fitted the temperature control lever on the heater panel should be in the right-hand or 'MAX' position.

IGNITION EQUIPMENT

Ignition adjustment

Adjustment is provided for the ignition point to enable the best setting to be attained to suit varying fuels. The adjustment nut is indicated by the lower arrow in the illustration below, and turning the nut clockwise retards the ignition. Turning it anti-clockwise advances the ignition.

The barrel of the screwed spindle has graduations to indicate the settings.

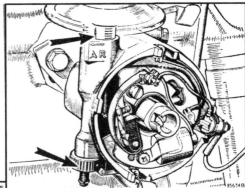

The adjustment nut is indicated by the lower arrow, whilst the other arrow indicates the vernier scale

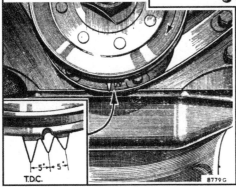

The groove in the crankshaft pulley and the pointers to assist correct timing. The long pointer indicates T.D.C.

Ignition setting

The normal ignition setting is with the spark taking place 7° B.T.D.C. The ignition point can be reset if necessary by adjusting the knurled nut on the distributor body. Each graduation on the barrel is equal to approximately 5° of timing movement and one graduation is equal to 55 clicks on the knurled nut.

Do not disturb the pinch-clip at the base of the distributor unless absolutely necessary.

Top dead centre

The rim of the crankshaft pulley has a small groove which coincides with the long pointer on the timing chain case when the crankshaft is in the T.D.C. position for Nos. 1 and 4 cylinders. The other two pointers are 5° and 10° B.T.D.C.

WIRING DIAGRAM (R.H.D. AND L.H.D.)

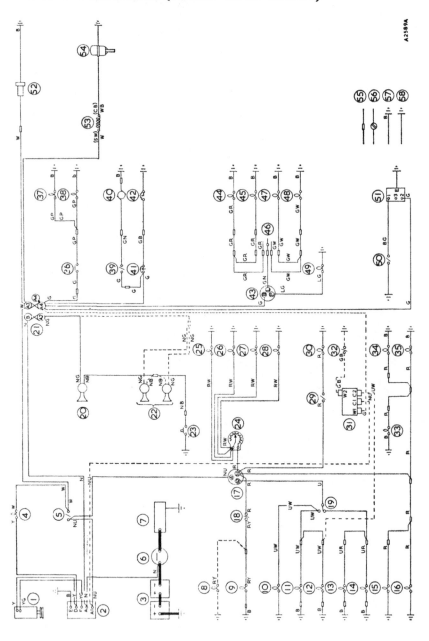

A2589A

22

KEY TO WIRING DIAGRAM (R.H.D. AND L.H.D.)

1. Generator.
2. Control box.
3. Two 6-volt batteries.
4. Ignition warning light.
5. Ignition switch.
6. Starter switch.
7. Starter motor.
8. R.H. fog lamp (if fitted).
9. L.H. fog lamp.
10. Main beam warning light.
11. R.H. headlamp main beam.
12. L.H. headlamp main beam.
13. L.H. headlamp dip beam.
14. R.H. headlamp dip beam.
15. L.H. pilot lamp.
16. R.H. pilot lamp.
17. Lighting switch.
18. Fog lamp switch.
19. Dipper switch.
20. Horn.

21. Fuse unit.
22. Twin windtone horns (if fitted).
23. Horn button.
24. Panel lamp rheostat.
25. Panel lamp.
26. Panel lamp.
27. Panel lamp.
28. Panel lamp.
29. Map lamp switch.
30. Map lamp.
31. Headlamp flick relay.
32. Headlamp flick switch.
33. L.H. tail lamp.
34. Number-plate lamp.
35. R.H. tail lamp.
36. Stop lamp switch.
37. L.H. stop lamp.
38. R.H. stop lamp.
39. Heater switch (when fitted).
40. Heater motor.

41. Fuel gauge.
42. Fuel tank unit.
43. Flasher unit.
44. L.H. rear flasher.
45. L.H. front flasher.
46. Flasher switch.
47. R.H. front flasher.
48. R.H. rear flasher.
49. Flasher warning light.
50. Windshield wiper switch.
51. Windshield wiper motor.
52. Fuel pump.
53. Ignition coil.
54. Distributor.
55. Snap connectors.
56. Terminal blocks or junction box.
57. Earth connections made via cable.
58. Earth connections made via fixing bolts.

CABLE COLOUR CODE

B. Black
U. Blue
N. Brown
G. Green

P. Purple
R. Red
S. Slate
W. White

Y. Yellow
L. Light
D. Dark
M. Medium

When a cable has two colour code letters the first denotes the main colour and the second denotes the tracer colour

ELECTRICAL EQUIPMENT

Batteries

Raise the hood and remove the spare wheel and hood stowage floor. The floor is secured by two quick-release screws.

Checking the specific gravity

Check the condition of the battery by taking hydrometer readings of the specific gravity of the electrolyte in each of the cells. Readings should not be taken immediately after topping up the cells. The hydrometer must be held vertically and the readings taken at eye-level. Check that the float is free and take care not to draw in too much electrolyte. The specific gravity readings and their indications are as follows:

	For climates below 90° F. (32° C.)	For climates above 90° F. (32° C.)
Battery fully charged ..	1·270 to 1·290	1·210 to 1·230
Battery about half-discharged	1·190 to 1·210	1·130 to 1·150
Battery fully discharged ..	1·110 to 1·230	1·050 to 1·070

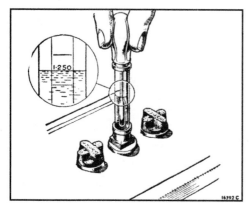

When taking hydrometer readings make certain that the float is free, hold the tube vertically, and do not draw in too much electrolyte. The readings must be taken at eye-level

These figures are given assuming that the temperature of the solution is about 60° F. (16° C.). If the temperature of the electrolyte exceeds 60° F. (15° C.) ·002 must be added to the hydrometer for each 5° F. rise to give the true specific gravity. Similarly, ·002 must be subtracted from the hydrometer reading for every 5° F. below 60° F. (15° C.). The readings for all cells should be approximately the same. If one cell gives a reading very different from the rest it may be that acid has been spilled or has leaked from this particular cell, or there may be a short circuit between the plates, in which case the battery should be examined by a Lucas Service Depot or Agent.

Top up the cells with distilled water. Do not use tap-water and do not use a naked light when examining the condition of the cells.

Do not overfill, and always wipe away all dirt and moisture from the top of the battery.

Never leave the battery in a discharged condition for any length of time. Have it fully charged, and every fortnight give it a short refreshing charge to prevent any tendency for the plates to become permanently sulphated.

ELECTRICAL EQUIPMENT

Fuses

Fuse connecting 'A1' and 'A2'

This fuse protects the accessories which are connected so that they operate irrespective of whether the ignition is on or off.

Fuse connecting 'A3' and 'A4'

This fuse protects the accessories which are connected so that they operate only when the ignition is switched on (stop lamps, etc.).

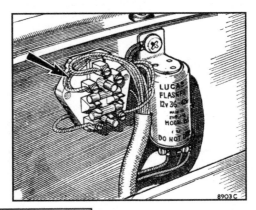

The fuses are carried in the separate fuse block mounted on the bulkhead

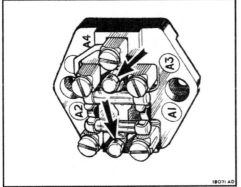

Two spare fuses are housed in holders on the fusebox

Spare fuses

Spare fuses are provided and it is important to use only the correct replacement fuse. The fusing value is marked on a coloured paper slip inside the glass tube of the fuse. If the new fuse blows immediately and the cause of the trouble cannot be found, have the equipment examined at a Lucas Service Depot.

Voltage regulator

This is a sealed unit located on the engine bulkhead which controls the charging rate of the dynamo in accordance with the needs of the battery. It requires no attention and should not be disturbed.

ELECTRICAL EQUIPMENT

Headlamps (except European type)

To reach the headlamp bulb remove the rim after extracting the retaining screw from the under side, push the lamp reflector and glass assembly inwards. against the springs, turn it anti-clockwise until the locating screws register with the enlarged ends of the slots, and withdraw the light unit. Depress the back-shell and turn it to release the bulb. When replacing the bulb ensure that the slot in the bulb flange engages the keyway in the holder.

To replace the back-shell push it home against the spring pressure and turn it to engage the bayonet attachment.

Refit the lamp unit by positioning it so that the heads of the adjusting screws pass through the slotted holes in the flange, press the unit inwards, and turn it clockwise as far as it will go.

Replace the dust-excluding rubber and refit the front rim, locking it in position with the retaining screw.

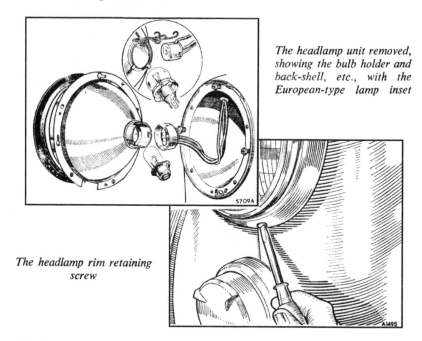

The headlamp unit removed, showing the bulb holder and back-shell, etc., with the European-type lamp inset

The headlamp rim retaining screw

Headlamps (European type)

The European-type headlamps are fitted with special front lenses and bulbs giving an asymmetrical light beam. Access to the bulb is achieved in the same way as for right-hand-drive cars, but the bulb is released from the reflector by withdrawing the three-pin socket and pinching the two ends of the wire retaining clip to clear the bulb flange.

When replacing the bulb care must be taken to see that the rectangular pip on the bulb flange engages the slot in the reflector seating for the bulb.

Replace the spring clip with its coils resting in the base of the bulb flange and engaging the two retaining lugs on the reflector seating.

Setting headlamps

The lamps should be set so that the main driving beams are parallel with the road surface or in accordance with local regulations. If adjustment is required remove the rim as described on page 26. Vertical adjustment is made by turning the screw at the top of the lamp. Horizontal adjustment can be effected by using the adjustment screws on each side of the light unit.

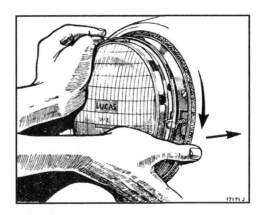

Push in the light unit and turn in an anti-clockwise direction to remove. Push in and turn clockwise (as shown) when replacing

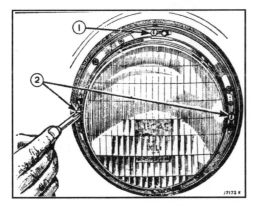

The method of setting the headlamp beams

1. Vertical setting adjusting screw.
2. Horizontal adjusting screw.

Remember that the setting of the beams is affected by the load on the car and the consequent spring deflection. The lamps should therefore always be set with the normal load on the car.

Avoid setting the main beams above horizontal; they will dazzle oncoming traffic and give inferior road illumination.

ELECTRICAL EQUIPMENT

Pilot and flasher lamps

To reach the bulbs push the lamp front inwards and turn it anti-clockwise until it is free to be withdrawn. Reverse the movement to replace the front.

Both bulbs are of the bayonet-fixing type and may be replaced either way round.

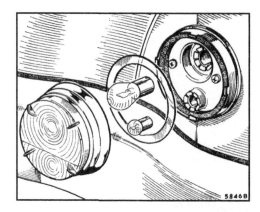

Push the lamp front inwards and turn in an anti-clockwise direction to remove

To gain access to the tail lamp bulb remove the two screws securing the cover and pull off the cover and rubber seal. Fold back the rubber flange on the flasher lamp to remove the lens

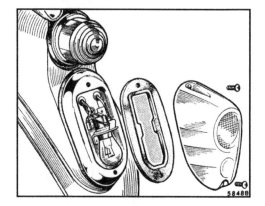

Tail, stop, and flasher lamps

Each tail and stop lamp cover is secured by two screws and the bulb is accessible after the cover and rubber seal are removed.

The dual-filament tail and stop lamp bulb must provide the brighter light for indication of stopping, and to ensure this the bulb has offset pegs and can only be fitted in one position. Fold back the rubber flange surrounding the flasher lamp rim to remove the rim and lens. Only the fingers should be used when folding back the flange.

Number-plate lamp

The number-plate lamp only operates when the sidelamps and tail lamps are switched on

A single bayonet-fixing bulb is fitted and the cover may be removed after slackening the small retaining screw.

Slacken the small retaining screw in the centre of the number-plate lamp to remove the cover

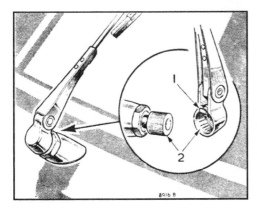

To reposition the wiper arm press the spring clip (1), withdraw the arm, and refit on another spline (2)

Windshield wiper blades

To reposition the wiped area on the glass the arm must be withdrawn from the spindle after pressing the spring retaining clip and then refitted on another spline.

To disengage a blade pull the arm away from the windshield and pivot the blade upwards.

When fitting a new rubber withdraw the old squeegee from the flexible carrier, taking care not to lose the locating pins.

ELECTRICAL EQUIPMENT

Jammed starter pinion

In the event of the starter pinion becoming jammed in mesh with the flywheel, it can usually be freed by turning the starter armature by means of a spanner applied to the shaft extension at the commutator end.

A jammed starter pinion may be freed by turning the armature shaft by means of a spanner

The location of the panel bulbs

Panel and map lamps and warning lights

There are four lamps illuminating the instruments, and their locations, together with the three warning lights and map lamp, are shown by the arrows in the accompanying illustration.

The bulbs are accessible from below the instrument panel.

Replacement bulbs (12-volt)

	Watts	B.M.C. Part No.
Headlamps (R.H.D. except Sweden)	50/40	13H140
Headlamps (R.H.D. Sweden—dip vertical—hooded) ..	45/40	3H921
Headlamps (L.H.D. Europe except France—dip vertical)	45/40	13H138
Headlamps (L.H.D. France—dip vertical—yellow) ..	45/40	13H139
Headlamps (L.H.D. except Europe—dip right)	50/40	13H141
Stop/tail lamps (irreversible)	6/21	1F9026
Number-plate lamp and pilot lamps	6	2H4817
Panel lamps and warning lights	2·2	2H4732
Flashing indicator lamps	·21	1F9012

WHEELS AND TYRES

Jacking up

Front

The screw-type jack should be placed under the lower wishbones with its pad engaging the depression between the spring seating and the lower link.

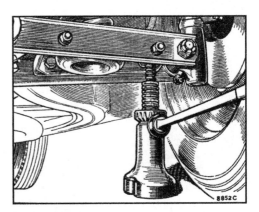

The lifting jack must be positioned under the front suspension arm between the spring seating and the lower link

The lifting jack positioned for raising a rear wheel. Place the jack under the spring as close as possible to the axle

Rear

The screw-type jack should be placed under the rear spring, close to the axle, when lifting the rear of the car.

Removing the wheel discs (pressed-steel wheels)

Remove the wheel disc by inserting the flattened end of the wheel nut spanner in the recess provided in the road wheel and levering off the disc, using a sideways motion of the spanner and not a radial one.

To refit the hub disc, the rim should be placed over two of the buttons on the wheel centre and the outer face given a sharp blow with the fist over the third button.

31

WHEELS AND TYRES

Removing and replacing the wheels (wire type)

Use the copper mallet provided in the tool kit to slacken the winged hub nut used to secure the wheel to its splined shaft. The hub nuts on the left-hand side of the car have right-hand threads (turn anti-clockwise to unscrew) and the nuts on the right-hand side of the car have left-hand threads (turn clockwise to unscrew).

Turn the winged hub nuts clockwise to unscrew on the right-hand side of the car and anti-clockwise on the left-hand side

Removing the road wheel securing nuts (pressed type)

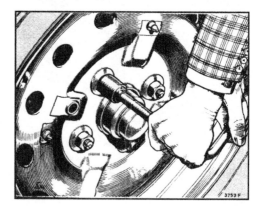

Removing and replacing the wheels (pressed type)

Slacken the four nuts securing the road wheel to the hub; turn anti-clockwise to loosen and clockwise to tighten. Raise the car with the jack (page 31) to lift the wheel clear of the ground and remove the nuts. Withdraw the road wheel from the hub, taking care not to lose the brake adjuster hole seal. When replacing the road wheel ensure that the correct hole in the wheel is in line with the brake-drum hole and that the securing nuts are fitted with the taper side towards the wheel.

WHEELS AND TYRES

Tyre removal

Inextensible wires are incorporated in the edges of tyres. Do not attempt to stretch the edges of the tyre cover over the rim. Force is entirely unnecessary and dangerous, as it merely tends to damage the cover edges. Fitting or removing will be quite easy if the wire edges are carefully adjusted into the rim base. If the cover edge fits tightly on the rim seating it should be freed by using the tyre levers as indicated.

Remove all valve parts to completely deflate the tyre and push both cover edges into the base of the rim at the point diametrically opposite to the valve, then lever the cover edge near the valve over the rim edge (see illustration below).

This permits the tyre valve to be pushed through the hole in the rim and the inner tube to be withdrawn for attention when required.

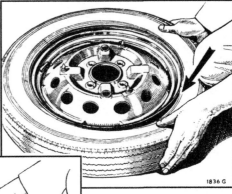

The cover beads should be pushed into the well-base of the rim opposite to the valve, as indicated by the arrow

The cover edge can then be levered over the rim close to the valve position to remove it, or replace it, as required

Tyre replacement

A similar technique has to be employed when replacing the tyre, first fitting the tyre into the rim at a point opposite to the valve and finishing the fitting in the region of the valve, keeping the beaded edge in the well-base of the rim.

Repairing tubes

Have punctures or injuries vulcanized. Ordinary patches should only be used for emergencies.

Vulcanizing is absolutely essential in the case of tubes manufactured from synthetic rubber.

33

WHEELS AND TYRES

Valve Interiors

It is advisable always to have spare interiors handy, and these are procurable suitably packed in small metal containers. A small extracting and fitting tool is supplied in the tool kit.

Always make sure that valve interiors are screwed well home on replacement.

Tyre valves

The airtightness of the valve depends upon the proper functioning of its interior. It may be tested for airtightness by rotating the wheel until the valve is at the top and inserting its end in an eggcup full of water. If bubbles appear the interior is faulty and should be replaced by a new one.

Checking tyre pressures

The tyre pressures should be checked and, if necessary, adjusted at least once a week. Gauges for testing tyre pressures can be bought from all reputable motor dealers.

The correct tyre pressures are given on page 4.

Valve caps

The valve caps should be kept firmly tightened to prevent dust and water entering and damaging the valve seats. The caps also act as an additional air seal.

When they are removed for tyre inflation or removal they should always be placed in a clean place.

Care of wire wheels

Wire wheels will require periodic checking to see that no spokes have worked loose or are losing their tension.

This can be done by drawing a light spanner or similar metal object across the spokes, which should emit a clear ringing note. If any spokes are slack the note will be dull or flat by comparison.

Any small amount of individual slackness may be taken up by adjusting the spoke nipple with a spanner, but great care must be taken to ensure the general tension of the wheel is not upset by overtightening any of the spokes as this will cause other spokes to break and the wheel to run out of truth.

If a spoke is replaced and it is found that the spoke end protrudes through the nipple body it must be filed off carefully to prevent any damage to the tube.

Tyres should be removed periodically so that the wheel rim can be examined for corrosion.

Any signs of rust must be removed by polishing with emery-paper and the area afterwards protected with paint.

When a general overhaul of wheels becomes necessary they should be sent to a wheel specialist for repair.

CARBURETTER ADJUSTMENTS

Adjusting the jets

Run the engine until it attains its normal running temperature and release the inter-carburetter throttle and mixture linkage. Set the slow-running screws on the carburetter throttle actuating levers so that the throttles are both open the same amount. This is indicated by the same suction noise at each carburetter.

Disconnect the mixture control wire from the end of the brass lever actuating the rear jet, and screw the jet adjusting nuts well downwards.

Note that the jet actuating levers must be kept in contact with the jet heads the whole time.

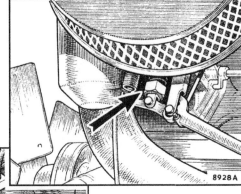

Each jet is adjusted by regulating the position of the large spring-loaded nut which forms the abutment for the jet head on each carburetter

When reconnecting the mixture control wire twist the inner cable slightly in a clockwise direction, looking at the end of the wire

The jet adjusting nuts should now be screwed upwards slowly (thus gradually weakening the mixture) until the engine idles evenly, firing on all cylinders regularly, and running at its best speed. This will be the normal slow-running position when the engine is hot, and as the jet needles are of the correct size the general performance on the road should be entirely satisfactory. Check by raising each carburetter piston with the pin provided beneath the dashpot flange. If the engine speed increases momentarily the setting is right. If the engine stalls the setting is too weak. If the engine speed increases permanently it is too rich.

The mixture control wire may be reconnected when the adjustment is satisfactory, care being taken to see that the control knob has ample clearance when the jet heads are in contact with the adjusting nuts. Final adjustment for slow running is then carried out by adjusting each of the carburetter throttle lever stop screws an equal amount before reconnecting the throttle and mixture linkage.

CARBURETTER ADJUSTMENTS

Slow-running adjustment

Before slow-running adjustments are attempted the nut indicated by the centre arrow in the illustration below should be slackened to allow each carburetter spindle to operate independently. Adjustment to the slow-running is made by resetting the position of the throttle lever stop screws, which are spring-loaded, until gentle slow-running is attained. When the slow-running is correctly set tighten the clamping nut on the interconnecting clip.

Make sure that there is a small clearance between the mixture and throttle interconnecting lever and its abutment screw.

It is important that both carburetters are set **exactly** alike, and you are advised to entrust this to an M.G. Dealer.

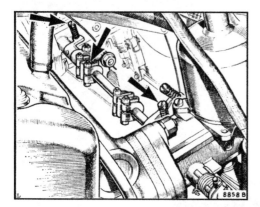

After slackening the nut indicated by the centre arrow the slow-running can be regulated on each carburetter by adjusting the two screws indicated by the outer arrows

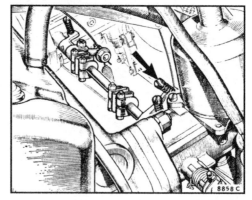

With the mixture control knob right home there should be a small clearance between the adjusting screw (arrowed) and the cam beneath it

Mixture control linkage adjustment

When the mixture control knob on the instrument panel is right home there must be a small gap between the adjusting screw and the interconnecting lever on the front carburetter. This gap determines the degree of interlinkage between the throttle and the mixture control and should be set so that there is just clearance between the end of the adjusting screw and the anvil of the rocking lever linked to the jet operating lever.

BRAKE ADJUSTMENT

Rear brake adjustment

Excessive brake pedal travel is an indication that the rear brake-shoes require adjusting. The brakes on both rear wheels must be adjusted to regain even and efficient braking. Block the front wheels and jack up each rear wheel in turn. Fully release the hand brake. Remove the hub cover (pressed-type wheels only) and rotate the wheel until the adjustment screw is visible through the small hole provided. Turn the screw in a clockwise direction until the wheel is locked, then turn back one notch only. The wheel should be free to rotate without the shoe rubbing. Adjust the other rear brake in a similar way. Adjustment of the brake-shoes automatically adjusts the hand brake mechanism.

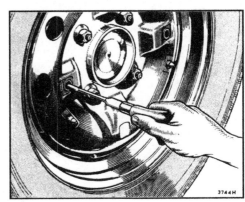

Access to the rear brake adjusting screw is gained through the hole provided in the brake-drum

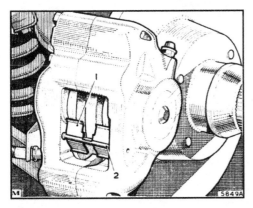

Press in the spring clip (1) and withdraw the retaining pin (2) to release the brake pads for examination

Front brakes

Wear of the disc brake friction pads is automatically compensated for and manual adjustment is therefore not required. The brake pads can be removed for examination by pressing in the spring clip (1) and withdrawing the retaining pin (2). When the lining material has worn down to the minimum permissible thickness of $\frac{1}{16}$ in. (1·59 mm.) the brake pads must be renewed. Special equipment is required, and it is recommended that the fitting of new pads should be entrusted to your M.G. Dealer.

FOLDING THE HOOD

Folding the hood

Never fold the hood when it is wet or damp—wait until it is dry.

(1) Release the hood from the top of the windshield.

(2) Release the rear of the hood from the three buttons and the turnbuckle at each side. Pull on the centre knob to release each button.

(3) Raise the front of the hood slightly to release the tension in the canvas, and pull the bottom of the hood to the rear to release it from the two anchor brackets above the luggage boot lid.

(4) Tip the seats forward, unfasten the sidescreen container, and turn it over onto the tonneau panel.

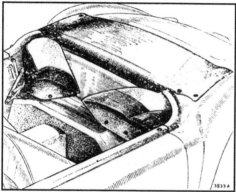

The hood is stowed in the compartment behind the seats

The hood is secured at the front by two wing bolts, which are slackened to release the hood. The clip at the top of the windshield in the centre must also be released

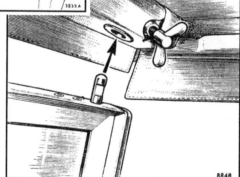

(5) Leave the rear window panel suspended over the body panel and collapse the hood into the stowage compartment, pulling the material clear of the hood irons and folding it over the front rail. Fold the rear window forward over the hood, pulling out the spare material at each side and folding it neatly over the front of the window.

(6) Push the folded hood well into the stowage compartment and bring the sidescreen container forward to cover the hood.

(7) Remove the sidescreens and stow them in the container pockets with the cranked bracket of each screen at opposite ends and facing the rear.

(8) Secure the sidescreen container over the folded hood with the six buttons.

SIDESCREENS

Sidescreens

The sidescreens are attached to the doors by means of a pin and socket at the rear and by a bracket at the front which is clamped in position by a pin and knurled nut.

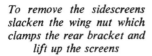

To remove the sidescreens slacken the wing nut which clamps the rear bracket and lift up the screens

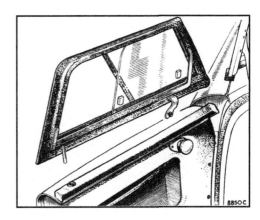

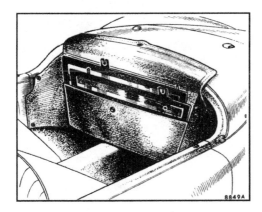

Stow the sidescreens with the cranked brackets at opposite ends

Sidescreen stowage

The sidescreens are stowed in a container behind the seats, and each should be placed in a separate pocket with the cranked bracket at opposite ends and facing the rear of the car.

MAINTENANCE ATTENTION

DAILY

Radiator

Check the level of water in the radiator, and top up if necessary.

Checking engine oil level (A)

The level of the oil in the engine sump is indicated by the dipstick on the right-hand side of the engine. Maintain the level at the 'MAX' mark on the dipstick and never allow it to fall below the 'MIN' mark.

The recommended lubricants are indicated on page 64.

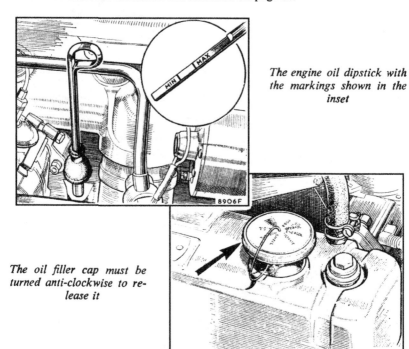

The engine oil dipstick with the markings shown in the inset

The oil filler cap must be turned anti-clockwise to release it

Filling up with engine oil (A)

The filling orifice is on the forward end of the cylinder head cover and is provided with a quick-action cap.

Clean, fresh oil is essential. The use of an engine oil to Ref. A (page 64) is recommended.

WEEKLY

Tyre pressures

Check all tyre pressures, using a tyre gauge, and inflate, if necessary, to the recommended pressures. Ensure that the valves are fitted with screw caps, inspect the tyres for possible damage, and wipe off any oil or grease.

40

EVERY 1,000 MILES (1600 Km.)

Gearbox (A)

When replenishing the gearbox care must be taken to ensure that it is not filled above the 'HIGH' mark on the dipstick. If the level is too high oil may get into the clutch case and cause clutch slip.

The combined filler plug and dipstick is located beneath the rubber plug on the gearbox cover.

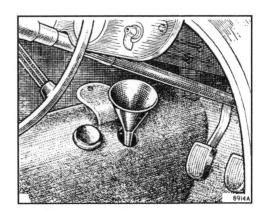

The gearbox oil filler is located beneath a flap and rubber plug on the gearbox cover

The rear axle filler and level plug

Rear axle (B)

Check the level, and top up if necessary. The filler plug is located on the rear side of the axle and also serves as an oil level indicator. After topping up allow time for any surplus oil to run out should too much have been injected. This is most important, as if the axle is overfilled the lubricant may leak through to the brake linings and lessen their efficiency.

NOTE.—It is essential that only Hypoid oil be used in the rear axle (see page 64).

EVERY 1,000 MILES (1600 Km.)

Carburetter dampers (D)

Unscrew the oil cap at the top of each suction chamber, pour in a small quantity of thin engine oil, and replace the caps. **Under no circumstances should a heavy-bodied lubricant be used.**

Failure to lubricate the piston dampers will cause the pistons to flutter and reduce acceleration.

An oil indicated under Ref. D (on page 64) should be used.

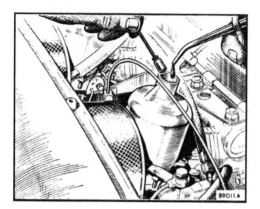

Lubricating the carburetter piston damper

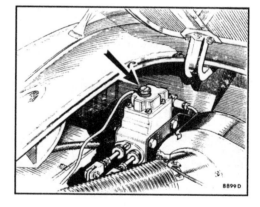

The combined brake and clutch master cylinder filler cap

Brake and clutch fluid

Remove the combined hydraulic brake and clutch master cylinder cap and check the level of the fluid.

The master cylinder is mounted on the driver's side of the dash panel below the bonnet, and the fluid level should be ¼ in. (6·3 mm.) below the bottom of the filler neck and never above this.

The use of Lockheed Genuine Brake Fluid is recommended. If this is not available an alternative fluid conforming to Specification S.A.E. 70.R1 should be used.

Steering gear (C)

Lubrication nipples are provided at the top and bottom of each swivel pin and on the steering tie-rods. The grease gun should be filled with lubricant to Ref. C (page 64). Three or four strokes of the gun should be given.

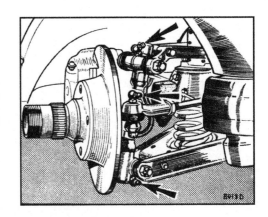

*The front suspension lubri-
cation nipples which require
regular attention. This illustration shows the right-hand
side only*

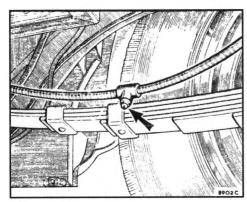

*A grease nipple is provided
on the hand brake cable and
will be found near the front
end of the right-hand rear
spring*

Hand brake cable (F)

The grease nipple on the hand brake cable should be given three or four strokes with a grease gun filled with grease to Ref. F (page 64).

Batteries

Remove the filler plug from each of the cells and examine the level of the electrolyte in each. If necessary, add sufficient distilled water to bring the electrolyte **just above the top of the separators.** Do not use tap-water and do not use a naked light when examining the condition of the cells. Do not overfill. Wipe away all dirt and moisture from the top of the battery. Refer to page 24 for further details.

EVERY 1,000 MILES (1600 Km.)

Propeller shaft (C)

Lubrication nipples are provided on the front and rear universal joints and also on the sliding yoke at the front end of the propeller shaft. Three or four strokes of the grease gun filled with lubricant to Ref. C (page 64) are required.

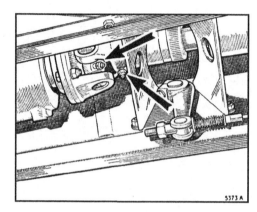

The lubrication nipples for the front universal joint and the sliding yoke

The lubrication nipple for the rear universal joint

Tyre pressures

Check the tyre pressures with an accurate tyre gauge, and correct when necessary. Do not forget the spare wheel, which should be maintained at the highest pressure recommended for the vehicle.

For a complete summary of the attention to be given every 1,000 miles (1600 km.) see also page 58.

Draining the sump (A)

Drain the oil from the engine sump and refill with new oil to Ref. A, page 64. The drain plug is on the right-hand side of the sump and should be removed after a journey while the oil is still warm and will drain easily.

The sump capacity is shown on page 4.

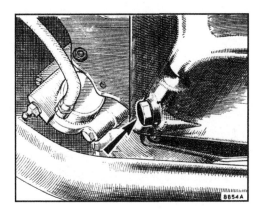

The engine sump drain plug is located on the right-hand side of the sump

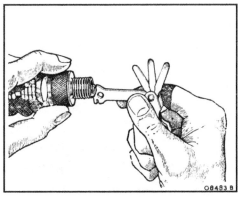

Use the special Champion sparking plug gauge and setting tool and move the side wire on the plug, never the centre electrode

Sparking plugs

The sparking plugs should be cleaned preferably by a service station with a special air-blast service unit, and the gaps should be reset to ·025 in. (·64 mm.).

Use the special Champion sparking plug gauge and setting tool and move the side wire on the plug, never the centre one.

Plugs which are oily, dirty, or corroded cannot give good results.

Fit a set of new plugs every 12,000 miles (19200 km.).

EVERY 3,000 MILES (4800 Km.)

Care of tyres

Every 3,000 miles (4800 km.) the running position of the tyres should be changed and the spare should come into use. This will equalize the tyre wear of the front and rear wheels and prolong the life of the tyres.

Inspect the tyres frequently and remove any pieces of flint, stone, or glass which may have become embedded in the covers.

See 'Front wheel alignment', page 53.

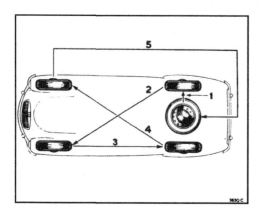

Change the wheels round diagonally and bring the spare into use as shown in this illustration

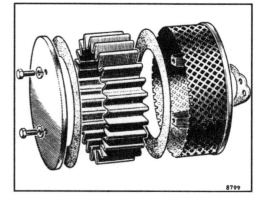

The components of the air cleaner are clearly shown in this illustration

Air cleaners (A)

Wash the filter elements in fuel and allow to dry. Re-oil the elements with S.A.E. 20 engine oil and allow to drain before reassembling.

When servicing it is only necessary to withdraw the two hexagon-headed screws and lift off the outer cover to release the corrugated element.

EVERY 3,000 MILES (4800 Km.)

Dynamo driving belt

Inspect the dynamo driving belt and adjust if necessary to take up any slackness. Care should be taken to avoid overtightening the belt, otherwise undue strain will be thrown on the dynamo bearings.

The belt tension is adjusted by slackening the bolts of the dynamo cradle and moving the dynamo the required amount by hand. Tighten up the bolts thoroughly, particularly the one passing through the slotted adjusting link (inset).

Slacken the two bolts attaching the top of the dynamo to the engine and also the two bolts securing the slotted adjusting link below the dynamo body when the belt tension requires attention

Front brake adjustment

Wear on the front disc brake friction pads is automatically compensated during braking operations; manual adjustment is therefore not required. In order to maintain peak braking efficiency and at the same time obtain the maximum life from the friction pads they should be examined at every 3,000 miles (4800 km.) service, and if the wear on one pad is greater than on the other their operating positions should be changed over.

This work should be undertaken by an Authorized M.G. Distributor or Dealer.

For a complete summary of the attention to be given every 3,000 miles (4800 km.) see also page 59.

EVERY 6,000 MILES (9600 Km.)

Draining the gearbox (A)

Remove the gearbox drain plug and drain off the oil.

When the gearbox has been drained completely 4 Imperial pints (2·27 litres, 4¼ U.S. pints) of oil to Ref. A (page 64) are required to refill it. The oil should be poured in through the filler plug shown on page 41.

The gearbox drain plug

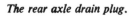

The rear axle drain plug.

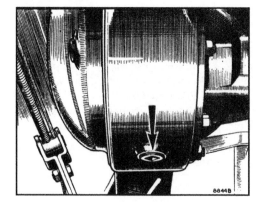

Rear axle (B)

Drain the oil from the rear axle and refill with fresh oil. The most suitable time for draining is after a long journey, whilst the oil is still warm. Clean the drain plug before it is replaced and tightened.

Approximately 2 pints (1·14 litres, 2·4 U.S. pints) of oil are required to refill the axle.

Distributor cam bearing (D)

Lift the rotor off the top of the spindle by pulling it squarely and add a few drops of thin engine oil to Ref. D (page 64) to the cam bearing. Do not remove the screw which is exposed.

There is a clearance between the screw and the inner face of the spindle for the oil to pass.

Replace the rotor with its drive lug correctly engaging the spindle slot and push it onto the shaft as far as it will go.

Distributor cam (F)

Lightly smear the cam with a very small amount of grease to Ref. F (page 64), or if this is not available clean engine oil can be used.

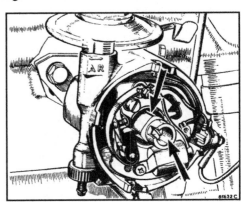

A slight trace of grease or engine oil should be applied to the rotating cam. The cam bearing should also receive a few drops of oil

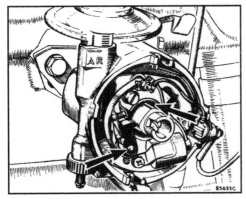

Lubricate the advance mechanism and the contact breaker lever pivot at the stipulated intervals

Automatic timing control (D)

Carefully add a few drops of thin engine oil to Ref. D (page 64) through the hole in the contact breaker base through which the cam passes. Do not allow oil to get on or near the contact. Do not over-oil.

Contact breaker pivot (D)

Add a spot of engine oil to Ref. D (page 64) to the moving contact pivot pin.

EVERY 6,000 MILES (9600 Km.)

Contact breaker gap

Check the contact gap with the gauge on the small screwdriver in the tool kit. Turn the engine with the starting handle until the contacts are fully open and the gauge should then be a sliding fit. If the gap varies appreciably, slacken the contact plate screw, insert a screwdriver in the cut-out, and move the plate until the gap is correct. Retighten the screw.

The correct gap is ·014 to ·016 in. (·36 to ·41 mm.) and the gauge is ·016 in. thick. If the contacts appear pitted or blackened they should be removed and cleaned with a fine carborundum stone or fine emery-cloth.

To release the contacts remove the nut, washer, and insulator from the retaining post and lift off the moving contact and the two insulating washers. Take out the two screws and remove the contact plate. Set the gap after replacing. Thoroughly wipe the distributor cap to ensure that it is clean.

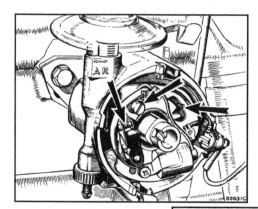

The distributor points, contact plate securing screw, and screwdriver adjusting slots are here indicated by the arrows

Remove the plug from the water pump and add a few drops of S.A.E. 140 oil

Water pump

Remove the plug on the water pump casing and add a small quantity of S.A.E. 140 oil. The oiling of the pump must be done very sparingly, otherwise oil will flow past the bearings onto the face of the carbon sealing ring and impair its efficiency.

Front wheel hubs (F)

Remove the front hub covers and carefully prise off the grease-retaining caps with a screwdriver (pressed wheels only). Repack the hubs with grease to Ref. F (page 64) and replace the caps.

To lubricate the front hubs on cars fitted with wire wheels the wheel-retaining nuts must be unscrewed with the copper mallet in the tool kit and the hubs packed with grease to Ref. F (page 64).

The rear hubs are automatically lubricated from the rear axle.

The front hub grease cap must be gently prised off with a screwdriver (pressed wheels only)

Unscrew the central casing bolt and the filter bowl may be withdrawn

Oil filter

The external oil filter is of the renewable-element type and is located on the right-hand side of the cylinder block. The filter is released by undoing the central bolt securing the filter body to the filter head. When fitting the new element make sure that the sealing washer for the filter body is in good condition and that the body is correctly fitted.

EVERY 6,000 MILES (9600 Km.)

Carburetter filters

To ensure a free flow of fuel to the float-chambers the filters should be removed and thoroughly cleaned with a stiff brush and fuel. Never use rag. The filters are situated behind the banjo-type union at the junction of the fuel pipe to each float-chamber lid.

Replace the filters with their helical springs first and their open ends outwards. Replace the fibre washers correctly.

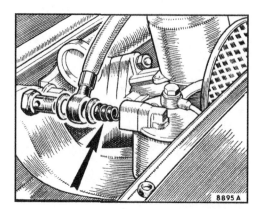

The carburetter filters must be replaced with their open ends outwards

Remove the hexagon plug at the base of the fuel pump and withdraw the filter

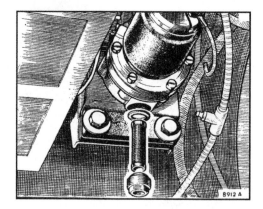

Fuel pump filter

Clean off the fuel pump, withdraw the filter, and clean it thoroughly in fuel. The filter is inserted into the bottom of the pump body and is released by unscrewing the hexagon plug.

When cleaning the filter do not use rag—always use a stiff brush and clean fuel. The fuel pump is fitted beneath the hood stowage compartment floor. Raise the hood and remove the spare wheel. The floor is removed by releasing the two quick-release screws.

Front dampers

Before topping up, the front damper bodies and wing valance must be thoroughly cleaned, particularly round the filler plug on top of the damper body.

When clean, the filler plug may be removed and the damper topped up to the level of the bottom of the filler plug hole. The use of Armstrong Super (Thin) Shock Absorber Fluid No. 624 is recommended for the dampers. If this fluid is not available a good-quality mineral oil conforming to Specification 20/20W may be used. This alternative is not suitable for low-temperature operation and is also deficient in various other ways. Rock the car before replacing the plug in order to expel trapped air.

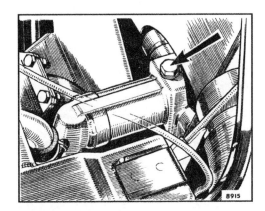

The arrow indicates a front damper filler plug. Thoroughly clean all around the plug before removing it

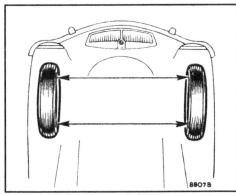

The front wheels should be parallel to each other when in the straight-ahead position

Front wheel alignment

Excessive and uneven tyre wear is usually caused by faulty wheel alignment. The front wheels should be set parallel, and care should be taken that the measurements are taken at axle level and that the rims run true.

Since correct alignment is so important and entails the use of a special gauge, this work should be entrusted to an Authorized M.G. Dealer.

EVERY 6,000 MILES (9600 Km.)

Valve rockers

Remove the valve rocker cover and test the clearance between the rocker arms and the valve stems by inserting a ·015 in. (·38 mm.) feeler gauge between them. The blade should be a sliding fit when the valves are tested in the following order while the engine is hot:

Test No. 1 valve with No. 8 fully open.
,, ,, 3 ,, ,, ,, 6 ,, ,,
,, ,, 5 ,, ,, ,, 4 ,, ,,
,, ,, 2 ,, ,, ,, 7 ,, ,,
,, ,, 8 ,, ,, ,, 1 ,, ,,
,, ,, 6 ,, ,, ,, 3 ,, ,,
,, ,, 4 ,, ,, ,, 5 ,, ,,
,, ,, 7 ,, ,, ,, 2 ,, ,,

The method of setting the valve clearance, and (inset) using a feeler gauge to check the clearance

To adjust the clearance slacken the adjusting screw locknut on the opposite end of the rocker arm and rotate the screw clockwise to reduce the clearance or anti-clockwise to increase it. Retighten the locknut when the clearance is correct, holding the screw against rotation with a screwdriver.

For a complete summary of the attention to be given every 6,000 miles (9600 km.) see also page 59.

EVERY 12,000 MILES (19200 Km.)

Rear dampers

It is not possible to top up the rear dampers in position and it is therefore necessary to remove them completely for cleaning and replenishing.

Clean the top of the damper and remove the filler plug. Top up the damper until the level is just below the bottom of the filler hole. The use of Armstrong Super (Thin) Shock Absorber Fluid No. 624 is recommended for the dampers. If this fluid is not available a good-quality mineral oil conforming to Specification 20/20W may be used. This alternative is not suitable for low-temperature operation and is also deficient in various other ways. Work the arm up and down to expel trapped air before replacing the plug.

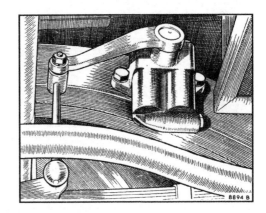

The rear dampers must be removed for topping up

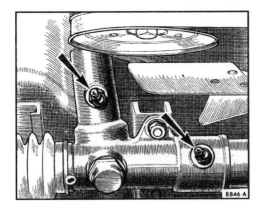

The arrow on the left of the illustration indicates the pinion nipple and the other arrow the steering rack nipple

Steering rack (B)

The two oil nipples for the steering rack and pinion are reached from beneath the front of the car.

Give the rack nipple 10 strokes **only** and the pinion nipple two strokes **only** with a gun filled with oil to Ref. B (page 64).

EVERY 12,000 MILES (19200 Km.)

Dynamo lubrication (D)

Add two drops of engine oil to Ref. D (Page 64) in the lubrication hole in the centre of the rear end bearing plate.

Do not over-oil.

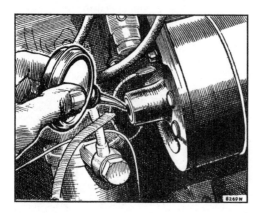

The lubrication hole for the dynamo end bearing. Do not over-lubricate

Engine-flushing (A)

Remove the engine sump drain plug and allow the old oil to drain completely. Replace the plug and pour in through the engine filler cap approximately 4 pints (2·27 litres, 4¾ U.S. pints) of flushing oil. A flushing oil supplied by one of the recommended lubricant manufacturers (page 64) should be used. Run the engine at fast tick-over speed for 2½ to 3 minutes. After stopping the engine special care must be taken to ensure complete drainage of the flushing oil.

Replace the sump drain plug and fill the engine with oil to Ref. A (page 64).

Sparking plugs

New sparking plugs should be fitted every 12,000 miles (19200 km.). Ensure that only the recommended plugs are used and that they are set to the correct gap (see page 45) before installation.

Speedometer cables

Every 12,000 miles (19200 km.) the speedometer outer casing should be unscrewed from the speedometer head and the inner cable extracted and lubricated sparingly with grease to Ref. F; oil must not be used. After returning the inner cable into its outer casing the upper end should be withdrawn approximately 8 in. (20 cm.) and the surface grease wiped off before reconnecting it to the speedometer head.

For a complete summary of the attention to be given every 12,000 miles (19200 km.) see also page 60.

BODY ATTENTION

Coachwork, wings, and windshield

Regular attention and care to the body finish is necessary if the new appearance of the car exterior is to be maintained against the effect of air pollution, rain, and mud.

Frequent washing of the bodywork, using a soft sponge with plenty of water containing a mild detergent, is recommended. Large deposits of mud must be softened with water before using the sponge. When clean, dry the surface of the car with a damp chamois-leather. Any damaged parts should immediately be covered with paint and a complete repair effected as soon as possible. When 'touching in' light scratches and abrasions with paint ensure that all traces of wax polish are removed from the affected area beforehand.

Methylated spirits (denatured alcohol) should be used to remove spots of grease or tar from the bodywork, windshield, and bright parts of the car.

The application of a good-quality liquid polish is recommended to give added lustre to the paintwork. Do not allow silicone- or wax-based polishes to come into contact with the windshield: they have been known to have a detrimental effect on the wiper blades and are difficult to remove.

Chromium and stainless steel

The chromium and stainless steel parts should not on any account be cleaned with metal polish. **Wash them frequently with soap and water,** and when the dirt has been removed polish the surface with a clean dry cloth, or a chamois-leather, until bright. The slight tarnish that may be found on stainless steel that has not received regular washing may be removed with impregnated wadding such as that used on silverware.

An occasional application of wax polish or light oil will help to preserve the finish, particularly during winter when salt may be used on the roads.

Interior

Clean the carpets in the car, preferably before washing the outside, by using a stiff brush or a vacuum cleaner. The leather or leather-cloth cushions and door trim may be cleaned periodically by wiping over with a damp cloth. Dust and dirt if allowed to accumulate too long will eventually work into the pores of the leather, giving it a soiled appearance that is not easily remedied. A little neutral soap may be used but detergents, caustic soaps, petrol, or spirits of any kind must not be used.

Hood

When necessary, the hood cloth may be cleaned with water applied with a brush without impairing its waterproof qualities.

Soaps and mild detergents may be used, provided the hood surfaces are well washed with water afterwards.

PERIODICAL ATTENTION

500 MILES (800 Km.) FREE SERVICE

During the early life of the car, soon after it has completed 500 miles (800 km.), you are entitled to have it inspected free of charge by the M.G. Dealer from whom you purchased it, or, if this should not be convenient, by any other M.G. Dealer by arrangement. This attention given during the critical period in the life of the car makes all the difference to its subsequent life and performance.

This service includes:

1. *Engine*
   Tighten cylinder head and manifold nuts to recommended pressures.
   Check tightness of valve rocker shaft brackets to recommended pressures.
   Check valve rocker clearances, and reset if necessary.
   Tighten fan belt if necessary.
   Check all water connections, and tighten clips if necessary.
   Examine and clean carburetters, and reset slow-running adjustment if necessary.

2. *Ignition*
   Examine, and adjust if necessary, sparking plugs and distributor points.
   Check working of automatic ignition control and, if necessary, reset ignition timing.

3. *Clutch*
   Check clutch pedal for free movement, and bleed if necessary.

4. *Steering*
   Check front wheel alignment and steering connections: adjust if necessary.

5. *Brakes*
   Check braking system functionally, and bleed lines if necessary.
   Check fluid level in master cylinder, and top up if necessary.

6. *Hydraulic dampers*
   Inspect hydraulic dampers for leaks.
   Examine oil levels, and top up if necessary (piston type only).

7. *Body*
   Check doors for ease in opening and closing.
   If necessary, lightly smear with a suitable lubricating agent all dovetails and striking plates.

8. *Electrical*
   Check electrical system functionally.
   Examine battery, and top up to correct level with distilled water if necessary. Clean and tighten terminals.

9. *General*
   Check tightness of universal joint nuts, spring clips, and wing (fender) bolts.

10. *Lubrication*
    Drain oil from engine, gearbox, and rear axle and refill.
    Oil and grease all points of car.

11. *Wheels and tyres*
    Test tyres for correct pressures.
    Check tightness of wheel nuts.

ALL MATERIALS CHARGEABLE TO THE CUSTOMER

Regular servicing, as proven by presentation of completed voucher counterfoils, could well enhance the value of your vehicle in the eyes of a prospective purchaser.

Daily

Inspect oil level in crankcase. Top up if necessary.
See that radiator is full of water.

Weekly

Test tyre pressures.

1,000 miles (1600 km.) service

1. *Engine*
   Top up carburetter piston dashpots.
   Lubricate carburetter controls.
   Top up radiator.

2. *Clutch*
   Check level of fluid in the hydraulic clutch and brake master cylinder.

3. *Brakes*
   Check brake pedal free travel, and report if adjustment is required.
   Make visual inspection of brake lines and pipes.
   Check level of fluid in hydraulic brake and clutch master cylinder.

4. *Hydraulic dampers*
   Examine all hydraulic dampers for leaks.

5. *Electrical*
   Check battery cell specific gravity readings and top up to correct level.

6. *Lubrication*
   Top up engine, gearbox, and rear axle oil levels.
   Lubricate all grease nipples (except steering rack and pinion).

7. *Wheels and tyres*
   Check tyre pressures.
   Check wheel nuts for tightness.

PERIODICAL ATTENTION

2,000 miles (3200 km.) service
Carry out the 1,000 miles (1600 km.) service.

3,000 miles (4800 km.) service

1. *Engine*
Top up carburetter piston dashpots.
Lubricate carburetter controls.
Top up radiator.
Check dynamo drive belt tension.
Clean and re-oil air cleaner elements.

2. *Ignition*
Clean and adjust sparking plugs.

3. *Clutch*
Check level of fluid in the hydraulic clutch and brake master cylinder.

4. *Brakes*
Check brakes, and adjust if necessary.
Change wheels round diagonally, including spare, to regularize tyre wear.
Make visual inspection of brake lines and pipes.
Check level of fluid in the hydraulic brake and clutch master cylinder.

5. *Hydraulic dampers*
Examine all hydraulic dampers for leaks.

6. *Body*
Lubricate door hinges, bonnet lock, and operating mechanism.

7. *Electrical*
Check battery cell specific gravity readings and top up to correct level.

8. *Lubrication*
Change engine oil.
Top up gearbox and rear axle oil levels.
Lubricate all grease nipples (except steering rack and pinion).

9. *Wheels and tyres*
Check tyre pressures.

4,000 miles (6400 km.) service
Carry out the 1,000 miles (1600 km.) service.

5,000 miles (8000 km.) service
Carry out the 1,000 miles (1600 km.) service.

6,000 miles (9600 km.) service

1. *Engine*
Top up carburetter piston dashpots.
Lubricate carburetter controls.
Top up radiator.
Check dynamo drive belt tension.
Lubricate water pump sparingly.
Check valve rocker clearances, and adjust if necessary.
Clean and re-oil air cleaner elements.
Clean carburetter and fuel pump filters.

2. *Ignition*
Check automatic ignition control, lubricating distributor drive shaft and cam and advance mechanism.
Check, and adjust if necessary, distributor contact points.
Clean and adjust sparking plugs.

3. *Clutch*
Check level of fluid in the hydraulic clutch and brake master cylinder.

4. *Brakes*
Check brakes, and adjust if necessary.
Change road wheels round diagonally to regularize tyre wear.
Make visual inspection of brake lines and pipes.
Check level of fluid in the hydraulic brake and clutch master cylinder.

5. *Hydraulic dampers*
Examine all hydraulic dampers for leaks and check fluid level in front dampers.

6. *General*
Tighten rear road spring seat bolts.

7. *Body*
Check, and tighten if necessary, door hinges and striker plate securing screws.
Lubricate door hinges, bonnet lock, and operating mechanism.

8. *Electrical*
Check battery cell specific gravity readings and top up to correct level.

9. *Lubrication*
Change oil in engine, gearbox, and rear axle.
Fit new oil filter element.
Lubricate all grease nipples (except steering rack and pinion).
Repack front hub caps with grease.

10. *Wheels and tyres*
Check tyre pressures.
Check wheel alignment.

7,000 miles (11200 km.) service
Carry out the 1,000 miles (1600 km.) service.

8,000 miles (12800 km.) service
Carry out the 1,000 miles (1600 km.) service.

PERIODICAL ATTENTION

9,000 miles (14400 km.) service
Carry out the 1,000 miles (1600 km.) service.

10,000 miles (16000 km.) service
Carry out the 1,000 miles (1600 km.) service.

11,000 miles (17600 km.) service
Carry out the 1,000 miles (1600 km.) service.

12,000 miles (19200 km.) service

1. *Engine*
Remove carburetter suction chambers and pistons, clean, reassemble, and top up.
Remove carburetter float-chambers, empty sediment, and refit.
Lubricate carburetter controls.
Check valve rocker clearances, and adjust if necessary.
Clean and re-oil air cleaner elements.
Check dynamo drive belt tension.
Lubricate water pump sparingly.
Clean carburetters and fuel pump filters.

2. *Ignition*
Check automatic ignition control, lubricating distributor drive shaft and cam and advance mechanism.
Check, and adjust if necessary, distributor contact points.
Fit new sparking plugs.

3. *Clutch*
Check level of fluid in the hydraulic clutch and brake master cylinder.

4. *Steering*
Check steering and suspension moving parts for wear.

5. *Brakes*
Check brakes, and adjust if necessary.
Change road wheels round diagonally, including spare, to regularize tyre wear.
Make visual inspection of brake lines and pipes.
Check level of fluid in the hydraulic brake and clutch master cylinder.

6. *Hydraulic dampers*
Examine all hydraulic dampers for leaks, and top up if necessary.

7. *Radiator*
Drain, flush out, and refill radiator.

8. *General*
Tighten rear road spring seat bolts.

9. *Body*
Check, and tighten if necessary, door hinges and striker plate securing screws.
Lubricate door hinges, bonnet lock, and operating mechanism.

10. *Electrical*
Check battery cell specific gravity readings and top up to correct level.
Lubricate trafficators.
Lubricate dynamo bearing.

11. *Lubrication*
Drain engine, flush out with flushing oil, and refill with fresh oil.
Change oil in gearbox and rear axle.
Fit new oil filter element.
Lubricate steering rack and pinion.
Lubricate speedometer cable.
Lubricate all grease nipples.
Repack front hub caps with grease.

12. *Wheels and tyres*
Check tyre pressures.
Check wheel alignment.

13. *Headlamps*
Check headlamp beam setting, and reset if necessary.

24,000 miles (38400 km.) service
Carry out the 12,000 miles (19200 km.) service, with the following amendment:

11. *Lubrication*
Remove engine sump and pick-up strainer, clean, and reassemble, filling with fresh oil.

Regular servicing, as proven by presentation of completed voucher counterfoils, could well enhance the value of your vehicle in the eyes of a prospective purchaser.

IMPORTANT

Your attention is drawn to the following points, compliance with which, we suggest, will prove mutually beneficial.

1. WARRANTY CERTIFICATE

(a) Completion of the Warranty Certificate 'tear-off' slip at the time of vehicle purchase when sent to the Factory will ensure registration of ownership by the British Motor Corporation.

(b) Retention of the Owner's portion of the Certificate, signed by the Distributor and Owner, in a safe place in the vehicle (by quickly establishing ownership) will help to expedite any adjustments under Warranty if such adjustments are required to be carried out by a B.M.C. Distributor or Dealer other than the supplier of your vehicle.

2. CLAIMS UNDER WARRANTY

Claims for the replacement of material or parts under Warranty must always be submitted to the supplying Distributor or Dealer, or, when this is not possible, to the nearest Distributor or Dealer, informing them of the Vendor's name and address.

3. PREVENTIVE MAINTENANCE

Service vouchers (applicable in the United Kingdom only) are produced for your convenience, and the use of these is the best safeguard against the possibility of abnormal repair bills at a later date.

Prevent rather than **Cure**.

4. REPLACEMENT PARTS

When Service Parts are required insist on genuine B.M.C. (MOWOG) Parts as these are designed and tested for your vehicle and in addition warranted for 12 months by the British Motor Corporation. ONLY WHEN GENUINE PARTS ARE USED CAN B.M.C. ACCEPT RESPONSIBILITY.

When purchasing replacement parts or having repairs done owners are requested to see that a label similar to the one illustrated here is attached to the invoice rendered. These labels are issued by B.M.C. Service Limited and constitute a guarantee that genuine B.M.C. parts are supplied.

Our world-wide network of Distributors and Dealers is at your service.

INDEX

INDEX

KEY TO RECOMMENDED LUBRICANTS

Component	A — Engine and Air Cleaner			Gearbox	B — Steering-box and Rear Axle (Hypoid Gears)		C — Lubrication Nipples	D — Oilcan and Carburetter	E — Upper Cylinder Lubrication	F — Wheel Hubs and Hand Brake Cable
Climatic conditions	Tropical and temperate down to 32° F. (0° C.)	Extreme cold down to 10° F. (−12° C.)	Arctic consistently below 10° F. (−12° C.)	All conditions	All conditions down to 10° F. (−12° C.)	Arctic consistently below 10° F. (−12° C.)	All conditions	All conditions	All conditions	All conditions
CASTROL	Castrol X.L.	Castrolite	Castrol Z	Castrol X.L.	Castrol Hypoy	Castrol Hypoy Light	Castrolease L.M. or Castrol Hi-Press	Castrolite	Castrollo	Castrolease L.M.
ESSO	Esso Extra Motor Oil 20W/30	Esso Extra Motor Oil 20W/30	Esso Motor Oil 10	Esso Extra Motor Oil 20W/30	Esso Expee Compound 90	Esso Expee Compound 80	Esso Multipurpose Grease H or Esso Expee Compound 140	Esso Extra Motor Oil 20W/30	Esso Upper Cylinder Lubricant	Esso Multipurpose Grease H
MOBIL	Mobiloil A	Mobiloil Arctic	Mobiloil 10W	Mobiloil A	Mobilube G.X. 90	Mobilube G.X. 80	Mobilgrease M.P. or Mobilube G.X. 140	Mobiloil Arctic	Mobil Upperlube	Mobilgrease M.P.
BP ENERGOL	Energol S.A.E. 30	Energol S.A.E. 20W	Energol S.A.E. 10W	Energol S.A.E. 30	Energol E.P. S.A.E. 90	Energol E.P. S.A.E. 80	Energrease L. 2 or Energol E.P. S.A.E. 140	Energol S.A.E. 20W	Energol U.C.L.	Energrease L. 2
SHELL	Shell X—100 30	Shell X—100 20/20W	Shell X—100 10W	Shell X—100 30	Shell Spirax 90 E.P.	Shell Spirax 80 E.P.	Shell Retinax A or Shell Spirax 140 E.P.	Shell X—100 20/20W	Shell Upper Cylinder Lubricant	Shell Retinax A
FILTRATE	Medium Filtrate 30	Zero Filtrate 20	Sub-Zero Filtrate 10W	Medium Filtrate 30	Hypoid Filtrate Gear 90	Hypoid Filtrate Gear 80	Super Lithium Filtrate Grease or E.P. Filtrate Gear 140	Zero Filtrate 20	Filtrate Petroyle	Super Lithium Filtrate Grease
STERNOL	Sternol W.W. 30	Sternol W.W. 20	Sternol W.W. 10	Sternol W.W. 30	Ambroleum E.P. 90	Ambroleum E.P. 80	Ambroline L.H.T. or Ambroleum E.P. 140	Sternol W.W. 20	Sternol Magikoyl	Ambroline L.H.T.
DUCKHAM'S	Duckham's NOL Thirty	Duckham's NOL Twenty	Duckham's NOL Ten	Duckham's NOL Thirty	Duckham's Hypoid 90	Duckham's Hypoid 80	Duckham's L.B. 10 Grease or Duckham's NOL E.P. 140	Duckham's NOL Twenty	Duckham's Adcoid Liquid	Duckham's L.B. 10 Grease

LUBRICATION CHART
KEY TO DIAGRAM

DAILY

(1) ENGINE. Check oil level with dipstick. Replenish if necessary with new oil (Ref. A).

EVERY 1,000 MILES (1600 Km.)

(2) GEARBOX. Check oil level with dipstick. Replenish if necessary with new oil (Ref. A).

(3) REAR AXLE. Replenish oil to level of filler plug hole. Use new oil (Ref. B).

(4) STEERING. Give three or four strokes with grease gun filled to Ref. C to nipples on steering joints.

(5) PROPELLER SHAFT. Give nipples three or four strokes with gun filled to Ref. C.

(6) HAND BRAKE. Give cable nipple three or four strokes with gun filled with grease (Ref. F).

(7) CARBURETTERS. Remove cap from each suction chamber and insert small quantity of oil (Ref. D).

(8) MASTER CYLINDER. Inspect fluid level in supply chamber, and refill if necessary with Lockheed Genuine Brake Fluid.

EVERY 3,000 MILES (4800 Km.)

(9) ENGINE. Drain used oil from sump. Refill to 'MAX' mark on dipstick with new oil (Ref. A).

EVERY 6,000 MILES (9600 Km.)

(10) DISTRIBUTOR. Withdraw rotating arm and add a few drops of oil (Ref. D) to spindle and also to advance mechanism. Smear cam and contact pivot with grease or oil.

(11) OIL FILTER. Renew element and wash bowl in fuel.

(12) GEARBOX. Drain used oil. Refill to 'HIGH' mark on dipstick with new oil (Ref. A).

(13) REAR AXLE. Drain used oil and refill to level of filler plug hole with new oil (Ref. B).

(14) WATER PUMP. Remove plug and add a small quantity of S.A.E. 140 Oil.

(15) FRONT HUBS. Remove front wheel hub discs and grease caps. Fill caps with grease (Ref. F) and replace.

EVERY 12,000 MILES (19200 Km.)

(16) STEERING. Give up to 10 strokes to nipple on steering gearbox and two strokes only to pinion shaft nipple with gun filled with oil (Ref. B).

(17) DYNAMO. Add two drops of oil (Ref. D) to oil hole in rear end bearing plate.

MULTIGRADE MOTOR OILS

In addition to the lubricants recommended in this Handbook we also approve the use of the multigrade motor oils produced by the oil companies shown in our publications for all climatic temperatures unless the engine is in poor mechanical condition.

NOTE.—Oil and grease references are detailed on page 64.

LUBRICATION DIAGRAM FOR THE 'MGA' 1600

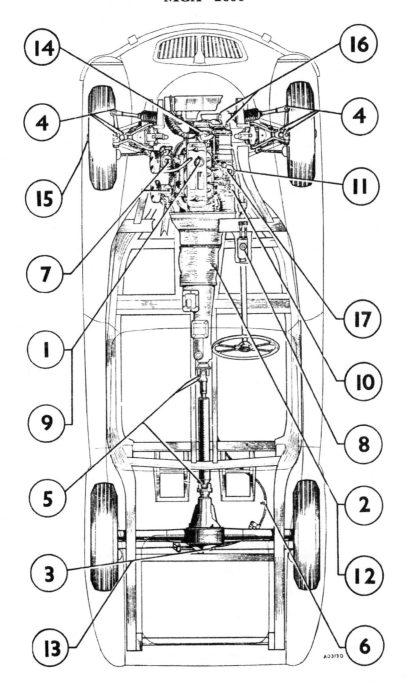

A03130

FROM BMC-FOR ONLY 65'-

Lap-and-diagonal-strap seat belt specially made for BMC by **Kangol Magnet Ltd.**

The seat belt a 2-ton tug can't break

☐ Approved to BSI Standard ☐ 100% Terylene webbing ☐ All metal parts non-corrosive ☐ Magnetic buckle release ☐ Simple single-handed adjustment ☐ Quickly fitted by your garage.

Get this remarkable new belt from your local BMC Service Garage
Also available—rear seat belts (£3.11.0) and automatic front seat belts (£6.0.0)

Manufactured by Britax (London) Ltd.

BMC SERVICE

Express... Expert... Everywhere

BMC SERVICE LIMITED · COWLEY · OXFORD

SERVICE

AUSTIN · AUSTIN-HEALEY · MORRIS · MG · RILEY · WOLSELEY · VANDEN PLAS

OFFICIAL TECHNICAL BOOKS

Brooklands Technical Books has been formed to supply owners, restorers and professional repairers with official factory literature.

Workshop Manuals

Midget Instruction Manual		9781855200739
Midget TD & TF	AKD580A	9781870642552
MGA 1500 1600 & 1600 Mk. 2	AKD600D	9781869826307
MGA Twin Cam	AKD926B	9781855208179
Austin-Healey Sprite Mk. 2, Mk. 3 & Mk. 4 and		
MG Midget Mk. 1, Mk. 2 & Mk. 3		
	AKD4021	9781855202818
Midget 1500	AKM4071B	9781855201699
MGB & MGB GT	AKD3259 & AKD4957	9781855201743
MGB GT V8 Supplement		9781855201859
MGB, MGB GT and MGB GT V8		9781783180578
MGC	AKD 7133	9781855201828
Rover 25 & MG ZR 1999-2005		
	RCL0534ENGBB	9781855208834
Rover 75 & MG ZT 1999-2005		
	RCL0536ENGBB	9781855208841
MGF - 1.6 MPi, 1.8 MPi, 1.8VVC		
RCL 0051ENG, RCL0057ENG		
	& RCL0124	9781855207165
MGF Electrical Manual 1996-2000 MY		
	RCL0341	9781855209077
MG TF	RCL0493	9781855207493

Parts Catalogues

MGA 1500	AKD1055	9781870642569
MGA 1600 Mk. 1 & Mk. 2	AKD1215	9781870642613
Austin-Healey Sprite Mk. 1 & Mk. 2 and		
MG Midget Mk. 1 (Mechanical & Body Edition)		
	AKD3566 & AKD3567	9781783180509
Austin-Healey Sprite Mk. 3 & Mk. 4 and		
MG Midget Mk. 2 & Mk. 3 (Mechanical & Body		
Edition 1969)	AKD3513 & AKD3514	9781783180554
Austin-Healey Sprite Mk. 3 & Mk. 4 and		
MG Midget Mk. 2 & Mk. 3 (Feb 1977 Edition)		
	AKM0036	9780948207419
MGB up to Sept 1976	AKM0039	9780948207068
MGB Sept 1976 on	AKM0037	9780948207440

Owners Handbooks

Midget Series TD		9781870642910
Midget TF and TF 1500		
Operation Manual	AKD658A	9781870642934
MGA 1500	AKD598G	9781855202924
MGA 1600	AKD1172C	9781855201668
MGA 1600 Mk. 2	AKD1958A	9781855201675
MGA Twin Cam (Operation)	AKD879	9781855207929
MGA Twin Cam (Operation)	AKD879B	9781855207936
MGA 1500 Special Tuning	AKD819A	9781783181728
MGA 1500 and 1600 Mk. 1 Special Tuning		
	AKD819B	9781783181735
Midget TF and TF 1500	AKD210A	9781855202979
Midget Mk. 3 (GB 1967-74)	AKD7596	9781855201477
Midget (Pub 1978)	AKM3229	9781855200906
Midget Mk. 3 (US 1967-74)	AKD7883	9781855206311
Midget Mk. 3 (US 1976)	AKM3436	9781855201767
Midget Mk. 3 (US 1979)	AKM4386	9781855201774
MGB Tourer (Pub 1965)	AKD3900C	9781869826741

MGB Tourer & GT (Pub 1969)	AKD3900J	9781855200609
MGB Tourer & GT (Pub 1974)	AKD7598	9781869826727
MGB Tourer & GT (Pub 1976)	AKM3661	9781869826703
MGB GT V8	AKD8423	9781869826710
MGB Tourer & GT (US 1968)	AKD7059B	9781870642514
MGB Tourer & GT (US 1971)	AKD7881	9781870642521
MGB Tourer & GT (US 1973)	AKD8155	9781870642538
MGB Tourer (US 1975)	AKD3286	9781870642545
MGB (US 1979)	AKM8098	9781855200722
MGB Tourer & GT Tuning	CAKD4034L	9780948207051
MGB Special Tuning 1800cc	AKD4034	9780948207006
MGC	AKD4887B	9781869826734
MGF (Modern shape)	RCL0332ENG	9781855208339

Owners Workshop Manuals - Autobooks

MGA & MGB & GT 1955-1968	
(Glove Box Autobooks Manual)	9781855200937
MGA & MGB & GT 1955-1968	
(Autobooks Manual)	9781783180356
Austin-Healey Sprite Mk. 1, 2, 3 & 4 and	
MG Midget Mk. 1, 2, 3 & 1500 1958-1980	
(Glove Box Autobooks Manual)	9781855201255
Austin-Healey Sprite Mk. 1, 2, 3 & 4 and	
MG Midget Mk. 1, 2, 3 & 1500 1958-1980	
(Autobooks Manual)	9781783180332
MGB & MGB GT 1968-1981	
(Glove Box Autobooks Manual)	9781855200944
MGB & MGB GT 1968-1981	
(Autobooks Manual)	9781783180325

Carburetters

SU Carburetters Tuning Tips & Techniques	
	9781855202559
Solex Carburetters Tuning Tips & Techniques	
	9781855209770
Weber Carburettors Tuning Tips and Techniques	
	9781855207592

Restoration Guide

MG T Series Restoration Guide	9781855202115
MGA Restoration Guide	9781855203020
Restoring Sprites & Midgets	9781855205987
Practical Classics On MGB Restoration	9780946489428

MG - Road Test Books

MG Gold Portfolio 1929-1939	9781855201941
MG TA & TC GOLD PORT 1936-1949	9781855203150
MG TD & TF Gold Portfolio 1949-1955	9781855203167
MG Y-Type & Magnette Road Test Portfolio	9781855208629
MGB & MGC GT V8 GP 1962-1980	9781855200715
MGA & Twin Cam Gold Portfolio 1955-1962	9781855200784
MGB Roadsters 1962-1980	9781869826109
MGC & MGB GT V8 LEX	9781855203631
MG Midget Road Test Portfolio 1961-1979	9781855208957
MGF & TF Performance Portfolio 1995-2005	9781855207073
Road & Track On MG Cars 1949-1961	9780946489398
Road & Track On MG Cars 1962-1980	9780946489817

From MG specialists, Amazon and all good motoring bookshops.

Brooklands Books Ltd., P.O. Box 146, Cobham, Surrey, KT11 1LG, England, UK

www.brooklandsbooks.com

ISBN 9781855201668   Part No. AKD1172C   1T14/2245   Ref: MG39HH

Printed in Great Britain
by Amazon

46378056R00040